George Alfred Townsend

The Mormon Trials at Salt Lake City

George Alfred Townsend

The Mormon Trials at Salt Lake City

ISBN/EAN: 9783743334359

Manufactured in Europe, USA, Canada, Australia, Japa

Cover: Foto ©ninafisch / pixelio.de

Manufactured and distributed by brebook publishing software
(www.brebook.com)

George Alfred Townsend

The Mormon Trials at Salt Lake City

THE

MORMON TRIALS

AT

SALT LAKE CITY.

BY

GEO. ALFRED TOWNSEND.

NEW YORK:
AMERICAN NEWS COMPANY.
1871.

LETTER FROM UTAH TO THE CINCINNATI COMMERCIAL,

OCTOBER, 1871.

———•———

Hon. W. H. HOOPER,
>   DELEGATE IN CONGRESS FROM UTAH TERRITORY.

My dear sir,

You wished to see the letters I wrote from Salt Lake last month, collected in pamphlet. Have your wish? Your courtesy and hospitality in the Land of the Bee, exercised in the two visits I have made you this year, were seconded by the best of the Mormon people. You are an Eastern Shore Marylander like myself, and I believe in your sincerity, in your faith and sympathize with your devotion to your beautiful country and the diligent hands which have made its deserts blossom. The march of the children of Israel from Egypt around the corner of the Mediterranean was a little affair compared to the Mormon migration. They were more unlettered and idolatrous than your bands, and Moses could not turn his back but they fell to worshipping calves and serpents. They conciliated nobody much on the way, and were a very unloveable, illiberal, rapacious set of people. They had awkward notions besides on the marrying point. And yet we, who are preached at from childhood out of the old books of Exodus and Deuteronomy, refuse to see any equities, wonders, or heroisms in the history and condition of a native church, whose legends are no less miraculous. I cannot confess to a deep interest in these ecclesiastical subjects, and your friends Orson Pratt and Dr. Newman appear to me equally fatiguing. But I do take pride in the material achievements of the United States, however brought about. Religious movements, however motley, have been the making of us. Amongst the names of John Robinson, Roger Williams, William

Penn, George Whitefield, Count Zinzendorf, and Lord Baltimore, founders of American communities, the name of Brigham Young will unquestionably stand. He has made the boldest, most rapid, and most remarkable colonization we have had; in a political point of view it has been fortunate to us all. I admire force of character and success achieved upon no baser principles than faith and industry, and I have said so in these letters. As to the camp-meeting jurists and their camp-followers out there, I am indifferent to their abuse and proud of their disapproval.

My friend, your people must stop polygamy, or it will stop Utah. Apart from the question of faith, it is a question of the common law. Your most generous apologists are only apologists, and they diminish in number every year. Do not tempt the democratic passions of a nation whose unanimous prejudice is law and power. Be rid of polygamy; cast out by this course the Federal officials who prey upon you, and become an American State in good faith, represented amongst us, and blessed by neighborhood rule.

                                        GEO. ALFRED TOWNSEND.

WASHINGTON, *November* 25, 1871.

THE MORMON TRIALS.

THE MORMON CITY AND CHIEF.

SALT LAKE, October 20.

THE train from the East has dashed down the wild, barbaric sceneries of Weber and Echo Canyons; and, although something of Asiatic inhospitality clings to the knobs and cliffs, we feel that we are approaching an oasis of grass; this grass we perceive by the quick tests of instinct, and it is confirmed by occasional kine and sheep; patches of cultivation slip into the inlets of ravines, and blue smoke appears to agitate the wheeling fishhawks; teams show upon the old stage road, useless now, except for neighborhood intercommunication. At last, with a whoop, brakes down, and the crack of rock echoes, the mountain gate yields; snow appears on distant ranges; there is something queer and blue hung across the dry sky—it is water. The Valley of Salt Lake, covered with cattle herds, and the town of Ogden, advise us that we are half way between the Missouri and the Pacific.

There is a darting about for baggage, many moving people and small traders, and a change of a few paces from depot to depot; in a little while we have paid our $2.50 in gold additional fare, and received in change queer, crude shin-plasters of the corporation of Salt Lake City, and are moving slowly over the Utah Central Railway, every employé of which is said be a Saint. This being the case, we feel no sense of personal responsibility, and so look out upon the green waves of the lake destitute of a sail, note the frequent Mormon hamlets, the close and snowy mountains sending down rapid torrents for irrigation, and seek to separate the sheep from the goats, the Saints from the Gentiles. In the last endeavor we unwittingly classify a methodist doctor of divinity as the possessor of four wives, and rate one of Tammany Hall's pilgrims as a Mormon bishop. Everybody looks queerly at everybody else, suspecting one another of the patriarchal virtues, and drawing many crude conceits of this or that innocent passenger sleeping all over his premises within the same small hours.

Finally, after more than two hours' ride we enter the environs of Salt Lake, among the small and bushy orchards of apple, pear, and apricot; the lean and often low, sundried houses, of a bluish-white color; and wide, straight streets, down whose lazy declivities the snow-water gurgles, passing at every other gate into the vegetable patches and the lawns of wheat and wild oats. A cleanly depot, well officered, gives us outlet to a street full of cabmen and hotel-runners. Cries of "Townsend House," "Salt Lake House," salute us, and a one-armed Mormon, possessing two wives, single-handed, cracks his whip, with the reins between his teeth, and makes the wagon fly. We see it all in a couple of minutes, the big temple, which resembles a tortoise standing on a hundred short legs, the ugly wall enclosing the palace of Brigham and the new temple, the lone theatre, the heathen-seeming city hall, the many shops, plastered in front with a monotonous signboard of "Holiness to the Lord," and one painted eye, winking at the motto as if to satirize it. Then we are set down at the "Townsend House," a long, low, sprawling hotel, with a comfortable piazza and shade trees, growing out of the wooden pavement. The only Townsend who can keep a hotel stands whittling a stick, and lazily counting the number of newly-arriven guests; it is apparent that his hostship sits heavily upon his shoulders. Townsend has three wives, originated in Maine, and is doing his best to multiply our great breed of freemen. We feed well at the Townsend House at $4 a day, and sleep in the delicious dry air of this Wahsatch Valley; and next day we take a warm sulphur plunge bath in the environs of the town, the hot water pouring from the mountain side into a pool, and a cold shower bath standing convenient, like an ice-cream at the end of a warm dinner. I observed in this bath-house and its dressing-rooms what was altogether exceptional in American out-houses—no vulgar writings on the wall, no sporadic bits of doggerel indited by cowards for women to read. The only attestations were testimonials in lead pencil to the pleas-ures of the bath, and the autographs of irrepressible travelers of vanity.

The valley and city of Salt Lake are marvels of patient, unskilled labor, directed by a few powerful native minds. The spirit of John Smith and the hands of the Puritan English meet in this mid-world colony—the brawn all peasant, the pluck all Yankee. Maine, Vermont, and New York were the fathers of this frontier, and folks out of the northwestern races of Europe—people of narrow foreheads and animal religious instincts— fell into the furrows the former opened.

The morning after my arrival I found everybody going up to see Brigham Young, some accompanied by an introducer, others falling in as interlopers. My *chaperon* was a bright young Mormon editor, as rosy as the sun on the mountains, who conducts a live salt newspaper, possesses a singular family, in that it is limited, and has built the first house with a Mansard roof in the heart of the continent. If he should feel distressed at any of these comments upon the Saints, my ingratitude will be great, and his paper will score me.

Passing under the small shade trees, across the flowing rills, past Godbe's flaming drug store, past Hon. Thomas Fitch's new law office, where he sits arranging his books with his cultivated wife; past the market where lake trout as big as young pigs lie speckled and fresh; past Delegate Hooper's bank, whence he looks out like one of Velasquez's Spanish gentlemen; past the chain-gang of worthless Gentiles making road with manacles dragging after them; past the theatre, and up a gentle hill among the painted adobe houses—everything flattish, low-set, quaint, but not permanent-seeming, as if all the town could be blown away by a gale— we see the sun shine hotly along the long, tall wall which encloses Brigham's palace. An eagle over a sunny gateway, a plaster or wooden bee-hive, and a lion above the roof, denote the clump of dwellings and offices just behind the wall, and seen through the gateway gap in it, where " President " Young keeps state. The scene is like pictures of scenery in Tunis or Morocco, hot, yellow, sandy, half-barbaric, as if architectural models were shaping themselves in a Darwinian way from the crude slime. He who would reign must not pick his palace, his capital, or his subjects.

A long procession of Eastern sight-seers is entering the gate, and amongst them are many fine young women, many wives, many young girls and children, and they pay as much respect to Brigham as to the Grand Turk. None of them appear to stand in dislike of him, because of his much marrying, and they push aside the Mormon brethren, who stand reverently off on the porch till the hand-shaking shall be done. It is truly queer to see that fine Boston belle, tall as a queen, with the rose and blush of maidenhood dignifying her for some impending husband, shake hands with the bland old Blue-Beard, whose honeymoons have been more numerous than her years. Meekly as Rebecca at the well she takes his palm, and looks honored by his consideration.

Within we see a snug office, narrow and deep, and in the recesses of it some secretaries, very like other folks' secretaries, writing. Everybody about Brigham, we may remark, is of a Gentile countenance and a worldly, business look; he does not take kindly to long faces; several of his confidential clerks have been associated with the Salt Lake theatre. This office is surrounded with portraits of the Mormon dignitaries, and it contains two large oil portraits—taken from life, as I was informed—of Joseph Smith and Hyrum Smith. Both wear clerical neck-ties and look like country clergymen.

How powerful is ignorance! See it tugging away at the Column Vendome, delighted with itself, noble and earnest, wiping out the monuments and vindications of our human nature, and sparing Heaven the necessity of humiliating us. Of all queer enterprises which ignorance has undertaken, Mormonism excels. It has not yet found itself out. With superb leadership, with patient delight, with prayer and praise, it goes on dignifying nonsense, and by its success almost making us infidel to our own religion and country; for what have we done in our knowledge that they have not imitated in theirs. Their humble apostles have passed the barriers of language, and the crude Danes and Swedes are pouring into Utah as well as the English-speaking nations. Compact, disciplined, devout, no cowards, at times desperate men, yet soft and diplomatic, so that they have pacified hostile Indians and checkmated the United States, they illustrate the nobility of delusion when attended with labor, fired with purpose, and properly organized. Moses, Roger Williams, John Brown, Joe Smith, very different, yet like in material results, the politician in all of them blended with the fanatic—they put in motion greater successors, and, by the two mighty inspirers of weak masses—sympathy and success—their sects grew to columns and their columns to States.

With his hair nicely oiled in ringlets and falling around his heavy neck, hair and beard luxuriant, and but a little turned in color, a pair of silver spectacles in his hand, and his manner all bland, from his half-closed eyes to the poise of his knees and feet, Brigham Young soothes mankind with seignoral hospitality. We are all introduced, except one young man, who steps forward and says:

"As there is nobody to make me acquainted, here is my card, President Young."

"It is unnecessary, sir," replies Brigham; "quite needless! Be seated."

We see he is more perfectly at home than anybody in the crowded room, and that he has a hard, peremptory voice, plausibly toned down to reception necessities. Looking not more than sixty years of age, he is past that period by half a score, and still may have twenty years to live. Of a wonderfully robust constitution, equal to all responsibilities of polygamy, of self-pride, cool self-management, and self-will, with an education chiefly religious, and an aptness and ardor for power and avarice. Young is wonderfully devised for organizing an ignorant and solemn people, and compelling them to be productive and docile.

About everybody of ecclesiastical prominence in the Church has several wives, and such bear themselves with added dignity. According to the number of the hens so grandiosely bears himself the cock, and I remarked amongst the most polygamous elders, that easy self-consciousness and grace of carriage becoming what are truly "ladies' men."

THE FIRST CONVICTION FOR POLYGAMY.

SALT LAKE, October 24, 1871.

To-day Thomas Hawkins, English, from Birmingham, better known around Salt Lake as "Tummus Awkeens," is to be sentenced in the best elocution of which Judge Mc-Kean is capable, to the Territorial Penitentiary for a term of years.

The offense of Thomas was somewhat uncommon—committing adultery with his wife, Elizabeth Mears, on complaint of his wife Harriet Hawkins, better known as Arriet Awkeens. He was also arraigned in the indictment for the same offense with his third and last wife, Sarah Davis, but no witnesses were adduced as to the criminal act, owing to the fact that Sarah quartered in the upper part of the house, and there was no way to observe what happened there, except by looking down the chimney. Voices, it is true, had been heard in that quarter, as of people sitting up or otherwise, toward morning; but it was somewhat singular that, although the first wife, complainant, had lived under the polygamous roof for several years, she swore that she had never beheld the direct offense charged but once, even with Mears, and then peeked in at a window on purpose.

As you are all anxious to realize this scene, I relate it below with all its atmospheric and personal surroundings.

"Hear ye! hear ye! The United States Court for the Third Judicial District of Utah is now in session. Hats off! Spectators will get off the jury bench!"

These were the remarks of the Deputy

Marshal Furman, who is intermarried with Mormons, but a prosecutor of the Saints, and brother-in-law of Billy Appleby, United States Commissioner in Bankruptcy. The Marshal, M. T. Patrick, had gone to Southern Utah to shoot snipe, prospect a mine, and arrest a Mormon Bishop.

The Judge on the bench, J. B. McKean, at once cleared his throat and looked over the bar and the audience. The Judge wore a blue coat, and was trim as a bank president. He sat upon a wooden chair behind a deal table, raised half a foot above the floor; the Marshal stood behind a remnant of dry-goods box in one corner, and the jury sat upon two broken settees under a hot stove-pipe and behind the stove. They were intelligent, as usual with juries, and resembled a parcel of baggage smashers warming themselves in a railroad depot between trains. The bar consisted of what appeared to be a large keno party keeping tally on a long pine table. When some law books were brought in after a while, the bar wore that unrecognizable look of religious services about to be performed before the opening of the game.

The audience sat upon six rows of damaged settees, and a standing party formed the back-ground, over whose heads was seen a great barren, barn-like area of room in the rear, filled with the debris of some former fair. One chair on the right of the Judge was deputed to witnesses. The entire furniture of the place might have cost eleven dollars at an auction where the bidding was high. The room itself was the second story of a livery stable, and a polygamous jackass and several unregenerate Lamanite mules in

2

the stalls beneath occasionally interrupted the Judge with a bray of delight. The audience was composed entirely of men, perfectly orderly and tolerably ragged, and spitting surprisingly little tobacco juice; almost all of them Mormons, with a stray miner here and there mingled in, wearing a revolver on his hip and a paper collar under his long beard.

At the bar table, on one side sat Baskins and Maxwell, the prosecutors, the former frowsy, cool and red headed, the latter looking as if he had overslept himself for a week, and got up mad. On the opposite side sat Tom Fitch, late member of Congress from Nevada, a rotund cosmopolitan young man, with a bright, black eye, a piece of red flannel around his bad cold of a throat, and great quantities of forensic eloquence wrapped away under his mustache. Behind him was A. Miner, the leading Mormon lawyer, turned a trifle gray, and thinned down in flesh very much since Judge McKean got on the bench; for the Judge uses Miner as the scapegoat for the sins of the bar, and threatens him with Camp Douglas and a fine every time he has a toothache. Whenever Miner gets up to apologize, the Judge makes him sit down, and when he sits down the Judge looks at him with his resinous black eyes as if he had committed solely and alone the Mountain Meadow massacre. Miner is the Smallbones of the Court, and is fed on judicial herrings. The other lawyers are all Gentiles, except Hosea Stout and one Snow, of the firm of Snow & Hayne,-a Vermonter. Yonder is a square-built man with cropped hair, ex-Governor Mann, Fitch's partner; they divide the leading business here, al-

though resident only six months, with Hempstead & Kirkpatrick, the former a slow,
serious military officer, and the latter a dark-
eyed Kentuckian. Kentuckian also is Marshall, the Ancient Pistol of the bar, rare and
stupendous in speech, and chiefly admired
by his partner Carter, from Maryland.
Marshall once did a good deal of Brigham's
business, but, with the impartial eye of a
lawyer, he afterward sued Brigham for Godby's fee, and lost the better client. Nothing
is a bereavement to Marshall, however, for,
as he frequently reminds the Court, the
jurisprudence of the country reaches its peri-
helion in the names of "Kent, Choate and
Marshall, of which latter I am a part."
Smith and Earl and De Wolf are about the
remainder of the Utah bar—a shrewd, clever
bevy of pioneer chaps, some of whom draw
large contingent fees from mining suits,
others encouraged to settle here by Brigham,
who does not like litigious emulation amongst
his own folks. He wants his good pleaders
to be preachers.

As Miner is the victim of the Court, the
Court in turn is the victim of Baskins, the
Prosecuting Attorney *pro tem.* Baskins
comes from Ohio, and gets his red hot temper
from his hair. He is related to have shot
somebody in Ohio, and about six months
ago he scaled the ermine slopes of Judge
Hawley, one of the three luminaries of this
bench. The Judge, by an order, came between Baskins and a fee. Baskins threw the
paper on the floor, and ground it with his
boot-heel into an inoffensive tobacco quid.
The Judge, who is slender, conscious, and
respects himself and his rulings, told Mr.
Baskins he would fine him.

"Go ahead with your fine!" said Baskins, "you're of no account."

The Judge fined Baskins one hundred
dollars, and sent him to Camp Douglas for
ten days. Baskins twitched the order out of
the Judge's hands and said that being an
"old granny" the Judge should forthwith be
kicked down stairs. At this Barkins threw
open the door to expedite the descent of the
venerable man, and rushed upon him, like
Damon upon Lucullus. The Marshal inter-
posed to save the author of so many learned
and long opinions, and Baskins went to the
Camp in custody. But as this notable Bench
in Utah never consult together, Strickland
agreeing with McKean in everything and
Hawley in nothing, Judge McKean let Baskins out on *habeas corpus* in four days, and
Baskins disdained to pay his fine. It is Baskins, therefore, who insists, as Prosecuting
Attorney, that the laws of the United States
and the Courts thereof must be respected in
Utah.

As for McKean's two Associate Judges,
they are off holding District Court at Provo
and Beaver, Hawley harassing some rural
justice of the peace with his last printed
opinion, and Strickland playing billiards for
drinks, between sessions, with Bill Nye. But
Judge McKean himself does not use tobacco
nor a billiard cue in any form; his sole re-
creation is to practice elocution and parlor
suavity in anticipation of his appearance in
the United States Senate from the State of
New York. A trim, apprehensive, not un-
sagacious man, with a great, burning mission
to exalt the horn of his favorite denomina-
tion upon the ruins of the Mormon Bishop-
rick, McKean is resolved in advance that

everybody is guilty who can keep awake under Orson Pratt's sermons.

There stand the guilty fold, without the bar of the court—most of them look as if they wanted a new razor and a square meal —the Mormon rank and file. Grave and listening, and so respectful as to irritate the prosecuting attorneys very much (so that they would like to make premeditated good behavior a conspiracy punishable at law), these Mormons, could they speak aloud, would swell a chorus profuse and unintelligible as on the eve of the miraculous Pentecost—Dane and Welshman, Norwegian and Finn, Westphalian and Belgian, hard, nasal Yankee, and wide-mouthed Northumbrian— lads from the collieries of Newcastle, the purlieus of London, and the mills of Bradford, they look upon the United States in a blue coat with a lead pencil in its hand as if it were the Man of Sin, and combined under the same baldish sconce the peculiarities of Guy Fawkes and Judge Jeffreys. Simple people in the main, who, with all their regard to the command to increase and multiply, feared the United States census takers as partners in their persecution, and cut down the returns of their population by sheer shyness, from 130,000 to 86,000 odd. Docile people, as well, though not without the courage of the poor, so that when on the late occasion of the great Methodist camp meeting, Brigham said to them in the Tabernacle : " I want you all to go to this camp meeting, and listen to what is said ! " they filled it to over-flowing every day, but the mourners' bench remained empty as a lion's platter. And when, on one occasion only, at some harangue upon polygamy, a mutter

arose over that great congregation, Brigham, himself present, stood up and waved his finger, and the complaint hushed to utter peace. People, also, who dance and waltz between religious benedictions, and yet can listen four hours in ardent delight to dry dissertations and discussions in their Tabernacle, which might make nature snore in her processes. How infinite are the possibilities of our nature when we reflect that these grave, unrebellious people, the waifs and findings of all lands, many of them dignified in apparel and culture, and steadily ascending in the scale of comfort and possessions, hold still with the tenacity of a moral purpose to the loose and spreading life of polygamy, preferring this fantastic reproduction like the Banyan's branches to the straight and peaceful unity of the European family. I saw in the court a Jew, lineal descendant of the old Patriarchs whom these Mormons delight to exemplify. His dark, shining eyes, aquiline beak, and wavy coarseness of hair made a strong contrast with those Saxon and Scandinavian races, fair-haired and highly-colored around him. He had marched down through two thousand years of wandering to accord with the century and Europe. And these Europeans had marched back six thousand years to resume the civilization the Jew had abandoned. What a feast for skepticism is this. But whoever looked closely could see the end of all this near at hand, unless fanned by irritation to fanaticism again. The weary faces, long and hollow, told of responsibilities too burdensome and of bodies overtaxed. The bright lights which shine in the face of him who submits to the life and customs approved by time and wisdom, were often darkened here. From the windows of the court, the rolling or serrated line of mountains, enfolding a valley like the lawn of Paradise, suggested far different men and women, and a life bounded by fewer necessities and wider opportunities for them all; a life consonant with the literatures of all these people, consonant with Christian art and promising a period of rest between labor and death. Who can look at this many-wedded manhood and envy it, or believe that its direction can be prolonged beyond the breaking of the darkness out of which this Mormon wife comes, like the feeble beam of the morning near at hand?

In a chair sat Mrs. Hawkins, a dark-haired, black-eyed woman from Birmingham, where she was converted to Mormonism about thirty years ago, and married to Hawkins, also a Mormon at the time, in an English parish church. Mrs. Hawkins wears a plain bonnet, a delaine dress, and drops her H's all over the floor. She refers to Hawkins as "my husband," and seems thoroughly aroused to the necessity of correcting him for the recreations of his maturer age. In short, Mrs. Hawkins has two suits against Thomas. This one is for adultery, and the next will be for divorce. Mrs. Hawkins is accompanied by her daughter, Lizzie Hawkins, a timid, embarrassed girl of about sixteen years, and while the mother is a prompt and rather bright witness, the daughter is measurably dumb. The daughter never saw anything wrong; she knew Elizabeth Mears' children were her father's, because they called him father, but she never saw anything in the Mears and Davis

end of the house, because she never went there except on a visit in daytime.

Thomas Hawkins looks like one who might enjoy married life, and yet be a rather mean husband. A square English head, bulging in the big, high, dwarf's forehead, plastered straight across from ear to ear with thin, long, yellow hair, which permits half his pale head to stand naked in front, and still be no bald-head; a light-blue, animal eye, which would pick out a woman quickest in a landscape; not an athletic body, and that clad in light, worn clothes; silent, attentive, and at times uneasy, during the trial—such is the meager hero of three marriages, brought up seven years after date to answer the charge of adultery. I have understood that Hawkins stands in doubtful odor among his church people for not equalizing himself more among his families, both socially and financially. The common expression among the Mormons is—

"There's wrong on both sides in that family;" but the inevitable addenda is—"just as in plenty of monogamous families."

Here is Mrs. Hawkins' testimony, in part, showing that all is not tranquil in those households, and that dissolution is proceeding of itself more rapidly than interference can promote it:

Q. Did you ever have any conversation with Thomas Hawkins on the subject of his living with these women in the house?"

A. Yes, sir.

Q. What did he say about it?

A. He said they were his wives.

Q. Did you ever have more than one conversation?

A. I have had many a thousand.

Q. State their substance.

A. Well, in the first place, he allowed he was doing religious duties, and he allowed that he had got to live with some one else.

Q. Did he give you any reason why he had to live with some person else?

A. Well, no reason; only he allowed that he had got to live with some one else! That I had had my day, and he had got to have some one else.

Q. Did you say you could consent to that?

A. No sir, I did not.

Q. What did you say to him?

A. I have told him that it was a damned bad trick, and that I did not believe in any such damned doctrine.

Q. Well, what did he say? What did he do?

A. Well, it didn't matter. If I didn't like it, I could do the other thing. He appeared to feel very indifferent about it, and I suppose if I had sanctioned what he wanted me to, and would have cleared out, that would have suited him, I suppose.

Miner Smallbones), the Mormon lawyer: You need not state what you suppose. State the facts.

Witness: I am speaking the facts. I am not to be insulted by you, Mr. Miner!

At this point, when it appeared to be coming out exactly how the inside of a heavenly mansion was conducted, and how objecting damsels were chastised, the lawyers made objections, and we returned to the matter of the adultery.

One other witness was called, the brother-in-law of Hawkins, who flew off in high dudgeon at the idea that a man's wife was "anything else" but his wife. *He* couldn't see any difference in the order of wives; 'e didn't know whether Mears was the second or sixtieth wife; it was none of 'is business, &c.

The audience laughed and applauded only once when Mrs. Hawkins testified that her husband's lawyer came to her to solicit a compromise, and said that unless she settled, the lawyers would get all the property. To this she replied that the lawyers might as well have it as "'is woman."

There seemed to be no feeling in the town except regret at the wife's suit for divorce, but a notion that the prosecution for adultery was malicious, and set on by the court and its favorite lawyers.

The oratory was mixed in the case. Maxwell, who was admitted at his own solicitation to assist Baskins in the prosecution, making the point against the Mormons that in twenty-two years their Legislature had never made a statute validating polygamy even by inference. To this Muller, the Mormon lawyer, replied that marriage was not a civil, but an ecclesiastical rite in Utah, that polygamy was established prior to the formation of any American government here, and relied upon a clause of the treaty of Guadaloupe Hidalgo, whereby the newly annexed inhabitants were guaranteed against interference with their religion The speeches of Maxwell and Baskins were bold and acrid, but the large Mormon audience listened without a murmur.

The reliance of the prisoner and his friends was upon Hon. Thomas Fitch, who came into the case late, and made an address which extorted admiration on every side, as well for its frankness as its legal incision. He is the best public orator and pleader west of the Rocky Mountains since the death of General Baker, and in the opening of his address he proclaimed himself an opponent of polygamy on every ground, and affirmed it to be a cruel and uncompensating system of barbarism, whether indorsed by former patriarchs or latter saints.

But the prisoner was on trial for adultery, and not for polygamy, and under a statute passed by a Territorial Legislature, three-fourths of whom were polygamists, and signed by Brigham Young himself, as governor, nineteen years ago. This statute fixes a penalty so severe as to show that the adultery meant was that committed outside, or in injury of the sort of marriage relation acknowledged here, prescribing from three hundred to one thousand dollars fine, and from three to twenty years imprisonment. To carry out its relentless purposes, this court—which had announced itself as a United States Court, and nothing else, and had quashed all territorial acts as to Probate Courts, selections of juries, divorces, &c.—now revives this obsolete statute, resumes for this object only a territorial jurisdiction, and punishes polygamy with the penalty of adultery.

Mr. Fitch's argument was that, as the Legislature had not defined adultery, the jury had a right to interpret the meaning of this statute according to the intent of the Legislature—the intent constituting the gist of the offense. The prisoner was clearly unaware that his offense was adultery according to any law enacted in Utah. The command, "Thou shalt not commit adult-

ery," was delivered to a polygamous people, and engraved upon stone by the husband of three wives. The same public opinion and religious inculcation which enacted the statute against adultery, married the prisoner to his wives, and honored the children of them equally. The rulings of the courts in Utah, both probate and district, for twenty years, had been in accordance with this theory of marriage, and now, seven years after committing the act charged with his second wife, "a rusty law is drawn from its antique sheath," and made retroactive upon this man. The polygamists on trial in the person of the prisoner had left civilized places and entered the desert, followed by the women, to attest their belief in this dispensation, and obey it out of the way of the people.

Here the eloquent advocate touched the audience to tears, and as he proceeded, an audible "boo-hoo" went over the court-room, two jury-men joining in the chorus, to the great alarm of the judge and Baskins, who feared that, unaware, some Mormons might have been insinuated into that packing-box. When Mr. Fitch concluded, there seemed a possibility, despite the clearness of Mrs. Hawkins' evidence as to the cohabitation between Hawkins and Mrs. H. No. 2, that the jury might hang.

To make this impossible, Judge McKean delivered a harangue to the jury answering every point made by the defense. It was a speech of three quarters of an hour, and amounted to an exhortation to convict. As to the intent of the Territorial Legislature, he said, that was no more to be conjectured than that *magna charta* could be interpreted

scarcely enough citizen material to get sufficient juries from it. The mines are ransacked to find people partial or ignorant enough to find verdicts according to the charging of the Court, and now the only reply the Ring makes to the allegation that they are without followers, is that the timid property-holders have fallen away from them. The Ring people, however, possess no property, unless "jumped" or prospective, and several of them are merely waiting for the spoils of violence.

Bishop Tuttle, the Episcopal functionary here, to whom Brigham Young gave a liberal subscription for the Episcopal Chapel, as he gave $500 to the new Catholic Church, is said to deprecate the precipitate action of the Court, as does Father Welsh, the priest. Dr. Fuller, ex-Republican acting Governor here; ex-Secretary and Governor S. A. Mann; Major Hempstead, District Attorney here for eight years, and even General Connor, an old enemy of Brigham Young, expresses contempt for these sensational court processes. Connor has just written a letter to Hempstead, saying that this action was altogether unfortunate as a repressory measure. The late Chief Justice, Charles C. Wilson, is even more pronounced in his condemnation of the Court. I. C. Bateman and D. E. Buell, as well as the Walkers, the latter the leading merchants of Salt Lake apostates, and the former two great mining capitalists, are said to be of the same mind. Joseph Gordon, late Secretary to Governor Latham, calls the Court hard names. The large law firms are nearly all in like attitude. Every Representative and Senator west of the Rocky Mountains, including, Cole, Williams, Corbett, Nye, Stewart, Sargent, and other Republicans, stand opposed to any measure which shall sacrifice Utah to blind bigotry without statesmanship. Mrs. Lippincott (Grace Greenwood), who is here, agrees with me in our mutual dislike of polygamy and of these "hot gospelers" and "notoriety hunters," who will not let it die ignobly, but must irritate it to renewed existence.

The original movement against the Mormons, through which the Salt Lake Tribune was started—the first paper here to attack the Church—began for quite a different interest. The valuable Emma Mine was then in litigation, and a decision of Judge McKean confirmed the Walker Brothers and others in the occupation and use of it, as against the claim of James E. Lyon, of Colorado. The Walkers occupied the mine jointly with W. M. Hussey, President of the opposition bank of Salt Lake, the Selovers, capitalists of New York, and Tranor W. Park, of Vermont, late financial agent of the John C. Fremont ring and candidate for the United States Senate from California. None of these wished to consummate the arrest of Brigham Young, or provoke any collision or debate in Utah, but they were forced to support McKean because his decision confirmed them in the mine. Meantime, Lyon and his attorneys, Stewart, Hempstead, Curtis J. Hillyer, and others, preferred charges against McKean, for his corrupt transaction in the Velocipede Mine, wishing to get him off the bench in the Emma Mine case. The Walkers and Hussey—to whom McKean was necessary—started the newspaper to sustain him, and McKean himself alleged that the Mor-

mons were behind the effort to remove him.
Thus the Emma Mine quarrel gave the anti-
Mormon ring a temporary appearance of
power which they no longer retain; for by a
compromise the mine has passed out of the
hands of the court, and Benjamin Curtis, of
Boston, has been made arbitrator between the
claimants, while the anti-Lyon interest has
relapsed to conservatism. So true is this
that the Salt Lake Tribune has ceased to be
the prominent ring organ, and they have
started the Review, to keep up the appearance of a quarrel here.

While the effort was being made to remove McKean, the Lyon interest called upon
Brigham Young to give it aid through his
great, but silent, influence in Eastern circles.

"No," replied Brigham; "whoever will
be sent here in his place will proceed to rob
and plunder us in the same way. I have
no choice between thieves, and can't help
you."

When the Emma Mine litigation, the un-
conscious entering wedge to Mormonism,
was pending, Tranor W. Park, who had
lived in Nevado, and knew the desperate
means often resorted to there to get ante-
judicial possession of a valuable mine, became apprehensive that Lyon and his lawyers
would import roughs from Nevada and seize
the mine by force. He cozzened Governor
Woods, therefore, for the sake of the military which Woods controlled, with the gift
of the presidency of a tunnel company, and
thus, perhaps, it happens that the Governor
is able to swear in one of his stock transactions, that he is now worth fifty thousand
dollars—either a large oath or a large commercial increase in a short while.

You can see from these data how much
more than the Mormon question there is
out here in Utah, and all the adventurers se-
crete themselves behind the halloo of "polygamy." No wonder the Mormons are
afraid of our judicial morals more than our
justice.

During the Emma Mine controversy it
is alleged that Judge McKean was afraid to
put Judge Hawley, his associate, upon the
bench in the Velocipede case for fear Hawley would grant an injunction upon the Park
interest working the Emma Mine.

The Velocipede case has been already
ventilated, and Senator Stewart denounced
the Court's transactions in it publicly in the
streets of Salt Lake. Here is the charge:

Judge Strickland, associate and crony of
McKean, "jumped" a mine in Ophir Canon.
Strickland sold his interest to McKean, who
organized a company called "The Silver
Shield," of which he was made President.
McKean retained Baskins, the Prosecutor of
Brigam Young, his attorney, and by visiting
all the lawyers practicing at McKean's Bar,
it was extorted from them that they would
not take the case against him. McKean then
commenced suit, in his own court, against
the original locators of the Velocip.de Mine,
and called Judge Strickland to sit in his
place.

The defendants declined to try the case
in the District Court before Strickland, on
the ground that he had sold McKean his interest, and was therefore as much interested
in the case as McKean himself. They ap-
pealed to McKean as Supreme Justice of the
Territory, to allow Hawley, the alternate
Justice, and who was disinterested, to try

the issue. This McKean refused to do; the case stuck fast in the courts; and McKean's company, the "Silver Shield," continue to draw ore from the Velocipede Mine, while Theodore Tracy, of Wells, Fargo & Co., and the Velocipede people, abuse McKean and Strickland without stint, and call them names not polite enough to put in this correspondence.

If the interior of a Mormon family is as tempestuous as a Gentile's out of-doors, the life must be worse than seductive.

The three men indicted by McKean's and Baskin's grand jury (the jury picked by Marshal M. T. Patrick, who has little or no sympathy with the court he must obey), Young, Wells and Cannon, are the vitality of the Mormon Church. Young is the organizer of the industry of Utah, and the ablest executive spirit west of the Rocky Mountains. His power is in his will, his Yankee materialism, and his position, now so long maintained as to be traditional with his people. They are proud of him, of his hale old age, fearlessness, sagacious enterprises, attention to their wants, and high rank amongst the great men of the time. He has brought the mass of them out of English, Danish and Swedish beggary, to a country of land, fruit, and scenery. He can put ten thousand men to work any day on his three railways, for their daily board, paying them wages in stock, and he needs no land grant or bonded indorsement. His enterprises generally pay speedy dividends. His tithing system brings out immigrants, who in time return the passage-money to the Church, and it reappears in large systems of mechanism and traffic. He has built five

hundred miles of the Deseret telegraph line, connecting all his settlements from St. George, where the Mormons cultivate cotton and mill it; past Provo, where a granite woolen mill, seven stories high, costing two hundred thousand dollars, and adapted to five hundred hands, is about to move its infinite spindles; up to Brigham city, where his narrow-gauge road is progressing toward Idaho. He has built sixty miles of coperative railway in Utah, one hundred and fifty miles of the Union Pacific Railroad, and many hundred miles of the Western Union Telegraph. There is no ecclesiastic in the Methodist or any other American church, with a tithe of his versatile and vigorous administrative ability. Of his sixty odd children, many are married to Gentiles, and all are endowed never with money, but with occupation. Brigham Young is still a credulous, sincere convert to the Mormon Church, and he has never pretended, himself, to receive a revelation. The church has made him, as well as he has dignified it; for he was only a painter and carpenter, with a serious nature, and an inclination for the Methodist Church, when the gospel of Joseph Smith overtook him, and drew him in. The prophet himself predicted a career for Brigham, and sent him abroad on a mission. Given thus a consequence and experience which old and beaten faiths would not have proffered, Brigham Young was ten years a traveling preacher and agent, and the doctrine of polygamy was no part of his suggestion. He accepted it as he did every other declaration of Joseph Smith; and the wife of his youth was dead before he ever saw the prophet. To this day, in all matters of mental erudition, logical analysis, and capacity to discover the illiteracy and mere cunning of Smith's writings, Brigham Young is grossly ignorant. As a theologian, he is only an exhorter and moralist. His life for all great ends began, not with education, but with a full superstitious conviction and entire allegiance to the Mormon Church. The mysteries of his faith he has never ventured to question, nor has he ever, with a learned man's skepticism, re-examined his creed. Such characters are common enough in other churches why not possible with this man whose life in all but polygamy has been abstemious, ardent and powerful, and who, considering his want of education, is, perhaps, the greatest living instance of human development without advantages?

Wells, the Mayor of Salt Lake, is a man of willing administration, entirely faithful to Young, in nothing else great, and he has a disagreeable cock-eye, but he is a diligent Mayor, and Salt Lake city is in much his creation.

Geo. Q. Cannon is one of the most intelligent Mormons, an Englishman and a good writer; outside of his family he is a pure man.

These three are selected for indictment upon the complaint of nobody but a grand jury picked especially with this object.

Bearing in mind these natures, strong men but zealous of forty years' standing (for Brigham was converted in 1832), you may imagine the situation when the indictment was served upon them.

There were gathered together in the Lion House Brigham's chief counselors : old John Taylor, who stood by Joe Smith when he

was shot in Carthage jail and was himself wounded, and would rather take his chances in the open air than go to a Gentile jail again ; a tall, good-looking, severe man with gray hair.

There was George A. Smith, cousin to Joseph, and, next to Young, the highest man in the church, also a witness of the sack of Nauvoo, a polygamist, but with few wives— a fat, aged, good-humored and rather weak Saint.

There was Orson Pratt, the chief theologian and expounder, whose brother, Parley Pratt, was shot dead by the Gentiles—a venerable-looking, Mosaic sort of man, with flaming beard, and large, introspective eyes, a Greek student, and a sort of Mormon Matthew Henry. The natty and flowery Dr. Newman, of Washington, who came out here with six Hebrew roots carefully committed to memory, expecting to demolish Orson with them, found the old fellow to be capable of talking Hebrew with Moses or Daniel.

There was Joseph Young, President of the Seventies, a lean face and low forehead, with a mouth like Abraham Lincoln's—elder brother of Brigham Young.

These and others, baked dry in the furnace of old Mormon dangers which they now account their glory, gave counsel to Brigham Young as to his duty. Almost unanimously they urged that he must never give himself up : the people would rise if he were to be convicted, whether he forbade them or no. Their counsel was to cut the irrigating ditches, burn every Mormon settlement in the Territory, leave the valley of Salt Lake in desolation, and march across

Arizona with their herds and portables to Mexican soil; these were their own, and they had a right to annihilate the property they had created.

Brigham Young, himself in the condition of an old lion, not uncertain that his prowess was now a part of his nature and religion, urged that he was promised safe conduct and fair treatment.

To this old John Taylor retorted: "So was Joseph! I saw the safe treatment they gave him in jail!"

There was a general exclamation of deep feeling and cry of perfidy at this,—and I am writing no fancy sketch, but the statement of two attorneys who were present. Brigham himself was deeply moved. Perhaps the recollection of his more youthful Captaincy of the Mormon exodus across the alkali plains inspired him with enthusiasm. To this urgent statement of the Gentiles that he could not hold out a week against the United States, the old man retorted with a strange, almost childish confidence, that if he were disposed to resist, the ally of Moses, of Gideon, and of David, would appear upon his side.

Then, after a minute, Brigham closed his great square mouth and jaw, and said calmly:

"God is in courts as well as in battles and marches. There will be no resistance. I shall obey the summons."

In due time he dismounted from his buggy before the little old squalid stone stable where the United States Court meets, climbed the creaky outside stairs, and at his colossal, venerable appearance, the whole Court unconsciously arose, bar and audience.

He was the overshadowing presence there, and when he answered "Not guilty," Judge McKean's elocution flew out of his head and he forgot, temporarily, to be dramatic.

INTERVIEW WITH THE MAYOR OF SALT LAKE.

SALT LAKE CITY, October 25, 1871.

Mr. Hiram B. Clawson, son-in-law of Brigham Young, and Superintendent of the great co-operative store at Salt Lake, said to me last night:

"D. H. Wells, a member of the first Presidency in our church, and the Mayor of Salt Lake City, wishes to state to you the distress under which we labor about our titles to property here. We have inhabited this place twenty-two years. Almost every other town in the territory has obtained its patents under the municipal town site act. But we, the oldest settlement in Utah, although Congress and the General Land Office have behaved with prompt liberality toward us, are so bullied and injured by Maxwell, the Land Register here, and the rest of these local adventurers, that we continue in only possessory rights, and we are annoyed by the entertainment at Maxwell's hands of every description of impudent and fraudulent claim. The Associate Press Agent here, one Sawyer, is under the thumb of the ring, and we have no means to communicate with our fellow citizens in the East."

"Do you suppose General Wells will talk upon other matters if I listen to him on this subject?"

"Yes. Anything legitimate. He is a bugbear to some people who don't know him, but you will find him, on contact, to be a simple, sincere, agreeable man, like any respectable American."

Soon afterward this celebrated Mormon warrior, the right-bower of Brigham Young, the Lieutenant General of the great Nauvoo Legion, numbering five thousand men, the commander of the Utah forces in the Sidney Johnston war, and the Fouchet of Salt Lake City, and terror of the criminals there, was ushered into my presence.

I beheld a tall, long-nosed, sharp-browed man, with gray hair, a tuft of gray whiskers on his chin and jaws, a bluish pair of eyes, one of them oblique and not prepossessing, and a bent back, the result of age and unrelieved labor. He would have been several inches over six feet high had he not stooped, but eminent service in the Mormon Church is of almost monastic rigor upon one so distinguished, and this old man had a way of winking which suggested eyes and head worn out in the Secretaryship of that mighty energy, "Uncle Brigham," while his clothing was poor and worn, and he talked with gentleness, almost like meekness. The Mormons have admonished me that, although he is a natural fire-eater and a military commander by instinct, he has latterly been a uniform counselor for peace and submission, and has helped to sway Brigham Young to wise advices.

As I never "interview" people off their guard, I took up a quire of paper and a pen, and made notes as the answers came to my questions.

The old man sat across the table, and his voice was seldom pitched higher than if he had talked to himself.

"My errand to you," began this gnarled old Mormon,—who was reared in St. Lawrence County, New York, and is an American typically,—"My errand is to relate to you the embarrassing—the needlessly embarrassing condition of our titles here.

"I am the Mayor of Salt Lake, and, as this was the first town settled in the Territory, I had an ambition to see it entered first among the town sites, according to general law. I made application, even before there was a Land Office opened at Denver, according to the prescriptions of the law of 1867, and followed it up respectfully and solicitously, when, in July, 1869, the Land Office was opened at Salt Lake.

"It is no fault of the United States Government that we are not now peacefully possessing the titles to the ground we have redeemed, and which Congress wishes us to retain. It is the fault of the unrelenting Land Register here, Maxwell, who has entertained and abetted every petty and malicious claim contesting our right to the site, and who hinders the entry of our city apparently with the object of being bought off or of discouraging us, or even of robbing us of it."

"How much do you claim as the proper area of Salt Lake City, General Wells?"

"About five thousand seven hundred acres, sufficient to give us water front on the Jordan and control of the irrigating reservoirs. We had laid out the city with an eye to coolness, breathing valves, wide streets and plats for recreations. The law is general upon the question of municipal sites. It gives three hundred and twenty acres to every one hundred people in a town; a town of five thousand people receives' four sections of the public lands. Salt Lake had grown so far beyond all precedents that we had to get a special relief bill passed, applying to our city, and we took a census for the purpose. The Land Office at Washington recommended and Congress promptly passed the special bill, under the terms of which we added to our original chart other essential bits of ground.

"What I wish to make plain to you is this: the nasty pretexts by which we are retarded in the matter of our entry!"

"Give me the names of all the claims which Maxwell has entertained against the city."

"Well, there are the Robinson, Slosson, Williamson and Orr cases. Robinson was a retired Surgeon of the Army, who kept a billiard saloon, and was a sporting man here. He jumped the Warm Springs property, our public bath-house on the outskirts of the town, with eighty acres of environing land, although we had walled up the spot, dammed the warm stream, fenced the inclosure, and used it so long under municipal regulations that the pump-cylinder with which we tubed the spring had rotted away. Robinson put a tent and a guard by the spring, and built a fence within our fence—a most impudent attempt to jump our property. We removed his obstructions, and he embarrassed us at law until his death, when his widow continued the suit, and the land agent actually permitted her to make a cash entry of the place. Very differently did the Washington authorities behave. The Commissioner of the Land Office decided without hesitation in

our favor, and the Secretary of the Interior confirmed it."

"What was the Slosson claim?"

"Slosson was a fellow who first rented a quarter section of ground from the city on the road leading to Camp Douglas, and when he undertook to keep a rum-shop on it in violation of law, we ejected him. He was then abetted by this Maxwell in a barefaced attempt to claim it and enter it; but Maxwell's decision was reversed by the heads of Department at Washington.

"The other two claims are even more preposterous, yet they are received and considered, and instead of disposing of them, Maxwell spends his time acting as volunteer counsel against us in criminal cases before the United States Court. Williamson jumped a bit of ground, claiming the pre-emption laws, and put a shanty upon it. It was a spot we had long previously reserved for a parade ground. J. M. Orr, a lawyer here, filed also Chippewa scrip for eighty acres between Ensign Park and Arsenal Hill, half-a-mile from the heart of the city. Now scrip can only take up land for agricultural purposes, and this claim is impudent beyond degree; but this Land Register entertains it, refuses to decide it, and so keeps back our entry. We are nearly, or quite twenty thousand people; our city is as old as many great towns in the Mississippi Valley; but here men are allowed to pre-empt farms right in the midst of us as if they meant to plow us under."

"What should I suggest, General Wells?"

"Why, the General Land Office ought to instruct this devilish Maxwell not to entertain these paltry claims, each of which is a

THE MORMON TRIALS.

reproduction of claims already thrown out. The Government means to encourage the formation and building of towns, but this agent vetoes the law in the case of the largest town ever established on the public lands."

[Here General Wells left me and went over to the City Hall, returning in a few minutes with copies of the Land Office decisions in the two cases decided, signed by Willis Drummond and affirmed by the Secretary of the Interior. These decisions state that "parties taking up land in the environs of town sites like Salt Lake City must take the risk of the lands falling within the town site," and that "where churches, schoolhouses, public buildings and places of trade and commerce are established in the form of a town, the land is already selected and held in reserve under the act, and cannot be infringed upon."]

Said General Wells: "We have no complaint to make of Congress or the Land Office in respect of our rights under the act. They have treated us well."

"As Mayor of the city, General Wells, do you meet with similar troubles in your municipal relations with the Federal Courts?"

"Yes. In the estimation of the Chief Justice of that Court there is but one crime in the world, and that is polygamy. There is but one set of criminals, and they are Mormons. He has mustered around him all the other vices, and adopted them as allies to move upon our one offense. Rum, prostitution, rapacity, incivility—these are the adherents of the Supreme Court of Utah in its holy war upon our marriage relation. The Court entertains every complaint made

against us. It gives Godby an injunction forbidding us to sue him as a corporation, and a score of unlicensed liquor dealers seem emboldened to defy us. The liquor sellers have now, I am told, by the advice of the satellites of the Court, raised a fund to sue the city when we interfere with them. The prostitutes newly landed among us rise up in that Court to assail our ordinances. The Court entertains every complaint, and those too preposterous to treat with seriousness it puts in its pocket and staves off, while crime takes advantage of the interregnum. Our Aldermen's courts have been delegalized, and we are told by McKean that a Legislature has no right to bestow discretionary powers on a jury or a civic corporation. In short, Mr. Correspondent, there is an end in Utah to any equality before the law. The end of the law is to reach polygamy. All are hailed as friends of the Government, however notorious, who will leave the great and decent body of the Gentiles and persecute us. Our Probate Courts are declared to have no power to grant divorces, and yet Mr. Baskins, the United States Prosecuting Attorney, is married to a woman divorced by a Probate Court. When Mr. Hawkins was sentenced for adultery, it is current that at least one man on the bench that sentenced him was guilty of that crime. But, then, we are Mormons! Finally, professional murderers like Bill Hickman are permitted to give themselves up by collusion with the Courts, and affect to turn State's evidence against us to prejudice us in the eyes of civilization."

"Who is Bill Hickman?"

"He is a Missouri desperado, who attached himself to our Church many years ago, and was turned out of it several years since. We have had him twice in custody for murder, and once, at least, the United States military authorities have taken him out of our hands. By occupation he is a cattle-stealer. He is the terror of the territory, and children are frightened at the menace of his name. Yet his evidence is admitted to prejudice respectable men in the estimation of their countrymen."

"Who arrested him?"

"One Gibson, one of the numerous deputy Marshals who have been sworn in from the lowest orders of society to overawe us. Gibson has been with Bill Hickman all summer, and there was probably an agreement between them."

"What does Hickman look like?"

"He is a thick-set, burly, sandy man with dyed beard, unable to look you in the eye. We took him up for killing a Mexican who had married his wife. He beat and deserted the woman, and she was divorced from him. He shot the Mexican dead in his doorway, and galloped off. Now, I am told, he is having his life written and embellished for sale. Since his incarceration he has taken to wearing broadcloth."

"Who was Yates, the man he swears he killed at the suggestion of yourself and others?"

"Yates was a trader of some sort whom Hickman brought to my camp in the Mormon war with a shackle on his heel. I ordered him released, and he wanted to go to Salt Lake, which was accorded him. He disappeared with Hickman and was never seen again. Hickman now swears that I said he was a scoundrel, and ought to be dead. Also that Joseph Young said he deserved death. What evidence to indict men of our age and position! I have no recollection whatever of the circumstances. They transpired fourteen years ago. Drown and Arnold were two other men whom Hickman confesses to have killed, and he implicates us there also."

[At this point I omit, and reserve for another time General Wells' remarks on the Nauvoo Legion and the military aspects of Utah.]

"General Wells, had you ever seen any military experience before you joined the Church?"

"No, except in the militia."

"How did you fall in with the Mormons?"

"Why, I had lived about ten years at a little place called Commerce, Illinois, and was a young man, Justice of the Peace there, when (in 1839) the Mormons were driven out of Missouri and came across Iowa to find a site for a settlement. They struck Quincy first, and scouted up the river to pick a place. Our town of Commerce was a 'paper city' only; the land was cheap, and we were not altogether sorry that the Mormons took it up. There were along about one thousand of them at first, and a poor, sick lot they were for several seasons. Joseph Smith began very soon to get up a memorial to the Government on the subject of the plunder of his people in Missouri, and they came before me to make their affidavits. Joseph Smith in person took those affidavits and the memorial on to Washington to President Van Buren, and I have often thought that the Mormon troubles began out of that errand of his."

" How, sir?"

" You see, a good many of the leading Mormons had, while in their Gentile state, been Democrats, among others the Smiths and Brigham Young. Joseph Smith expected that Van Buren would recognize him to some degree because of their predilections for the same party, but when he presented his case Van Buren made this unsatisfactory reply : 'Your cause is just, but I cannot help you. Address your story to the magnanimous State and people of Missouri.' When Joseph Smith returned to Nauvoo he told his people to vote for Harrison in 1840, which they did solidly, and this irritated the Democrats, who counted upon the Mormon vote. Afterwards, Joseph directed his people to vote for men friendly to them rather than for mere parties. The idea got abroad, after awhile, that the Mormons could not be counted upon politically by either side, and it got to be a notion among the Illinois vote-getters that they could intimidate these poor people against supporting the opposite side. The intimidation thus begun led to the mob spirit, which sacrificed Joseph in 1844.

"I was a Whig, and I thought the Mormons were sometimees as far wrong as their enemies, but I could not shut my eyes to the fact that even my party did not treat them like human creatures. I remember well that among my Whig acquaintances was a well-reared young man, named Morrison. He said to me one day : 'By God! we mean to make them vote our ticket this year. The Democrats forced them to support theirs last year, and we can do the same thing this time.'

"'How?' said I.

"'Well. We'll get a requisition from the Governor of Missouri for Joe Smith and we'll hold that requisition over his head and force him to give us the votes of all his crowd or serve it on him.'

"This looked like a mean trick to me, and I found myself, perhaps out of natural combativeness, standing between the Mormons and their persecutors, and finally, after a good deal of consideration, I joined the Church, several years after my acquaintance with the leaders."

"What was the origin of the word, Nauvoo?"

"They say it meant in Hebrew, 'beautiful site' or 'beautiful city.' I know nothing of Hebrew and can't tell whether that is true or not."

"General, what became of Sidney Rigdon, Joseph's early coadjutor?"

"Well, he is living now at Friendship, a town I think in Western New York, near Buffalo. He took it to heart that he was not promoted in the Church, and left us; at present he is a very old, pusillanimous man, who sometimes addresses us communications. He offered at one time to guarantee us the protection of Providence if we would make up one hundred thousand dollars for him, and still later we hear that he has predicted our early overthrow."

"He has been supposed by some to have been Joseph's intellectual and executive superior, and to have given Mormonism its original impetus?"

"Oh, no. Joseph was the man. Oliver Cowdrey, an educated person, was of more assistance to Joseph than Rigdon; for he wrote a good hand and acted as Joseph's Secretary, Smith himself being at first illite- rate, unable to write, and obliged to confine his correspondence to dictation. However, Joseph burnished up greatly in the fourteen years of his Presidency; such trials as his would educate almost any man."

"Is Cowdrey living?"

"No. He left the Church while we were still at Nauvoo; then he repented and followed us across the plains, and was re- baptized and received into fellowship. Pay- ing a visit or going upon a mission to Mis- souri, he was taken sick and died there."

"What was the fate of Joseph's refrac- tory wife, Emma Smith?"

"She, like Rigdon, was dissatisfied with the amount of consideration she received in the Church after Joseph's death, and would not come with us, but remained in Illinois, near Nauvoo, and I understand that she mar- ried another husband and is living there now."

"Have you ever visited Nauvoo since the exodus in 1846?"

"No, sir; not since the destruction of the temple. President Young appointed me Adjutant to keep the emigrant and supply teams well up through Iowa, and afterward across the Plains. I remember that when we had crossed the Mississippi upon impro- vised rafts, floats and boats, the poorest and most despairing body of halt, lame, sick and uncertain people you ever saw in the world —that the military mob marched up in front of the temple, planted a cannon and fired across into our camps of sick, adding panic to wretchedness. All that is past and for- gotten with us, but it is accurately set down

in our church history, and we got converts all around the country, from among the wit- nesses of those scenes."

"Where is Joseph's body buried?"

"At Nauvoo. It was buried secretly. He was shot in several places in the breast, if I remember well, and Hyrum Smith was shot in the face. I was not present at Car- thage at the massacre, but around Nauvoo I saw many frightful scenes, which confirmed me in my already half-formed idea that these Mormons were a persecuted people and bet- ter Christians than my neighbors. The mob used to get in the bushes, for instance, on the out skirts of Nauvoo, set a man's barn or haystack a fire, and then by the light of the blaze shoot him as he ran away."

"Are those good pictures of Joseph and Hyrum Smith at President Young's office?"

"Yes; good likenesses. Hyrum was the devoted brother of Joseph, believed in him from the first, kept with him all the way down, and they died together, as I had seen them a many hundred times, walking fondly side by side. Brigham Young, also, was a bosom friend of Joseph Smith, and an emi- nent man in the Church at that early day. He was President of the Quorum of the Twelve Apostles."

"Can you give me an idea of Joseph Smith, so that I can realize him?"

"He was a large man, weighing two hun- dred pounds, and about six feet high, with a countenance never sanctimonious, but always cheerful and bright; brown hair and light eyes, and I might call him a real jam-up free-and-easy good fellow. He used to play ball, run and wrestle with the people, and if a big man joined the Church, Joseph would pick him out and try him for a throw, for he had a conceit that he was a match for 'most anybody.' You can see that we keep up in the Church his example of liveliness in our theater and Social Hall."

"Was it at Nauvoo that Joseph proclaimed the revelation of polygamy?"

"Oh, no. He had received it a long while before his death, and his counselors knew of it, but he was afraid to make it public."

"General Wells, is it true that the officers of the Mormon Church are elected frequently, and that they all owe their offices to popular will?"

"Yes, sir. We have two annual conferences, one meeting on the 6th of April, the day our church was organized in the year 1830, and the other on the 6th of October. Each conference continues in session from four days to a week, and all the people of the Territory come up, frequently twelve thousand people assembling in the big Tabernacle. Every member, man and woman, has a vote. I have myself been discontinued of my office, on at least, one occasion. Brigham Young has to be elected separately to each and every office he holds, first President, Trustee, &c. As our people willingly respect their authorities, the nominations made by the higher quorums are generally confirmed, but it is anybody's province to disagree. The Methodist Church is not as liberal as ours in ecclesiastical discipline. It sends its clergymen from post to pillar *willy-nilly*, and refuses its membership a share in their own government. Its chief functionaries are elected once and for life, and the Church subsists largely upon non-communi-

cants, seeking aid and extension promiscuously. We live within our membership; our tithing system, so much decried, is consonant with the general inculcations of the Gospel, to give one-tenth of our substance to charity and religion.

"The Methodist Church teaches in its Discipline or manual of government, the Christian duty of every communicant to employ his brother and deal with his sect, and it enjoins upon each Methodist not to sue another Methodist at law until the board of Stewards, Trustees, or whatever it is, have first tried to arbitrate in the case.

"We accepted a debate with a preacher of the Methodist Church last year, and our people had no reason to be ashamed of the argument; but since that time the Methodist, who were worsted, have undertaken a regular war at law against us. It behooves them to republicanize their Church before they assail ours."

"General Wells, I wish you would tell me what it was that began the Mormon war of 1857."

"I can answer that in one word—Bill Drummond!"

"Who was he?"

"One of the United States Judges. He came here from Illinois and spent most of his time at the town of Fillmore. There were frequent rows at his Court, resembling McKean's wranglings with us at present, but we did not know that he was backed up by the Government, and we set his attitude down to general personal 'cussedness.' He wanted to be transferred to another Court, it seems, nearer the Pacific coast, and thought before leaving us that he would fire a parting shot. So after he slipped away, there appeared at Washington a report, signed by him, charging us with every sort of crime, and this was immediately followed by a general yell from the newspaper press.

"As we had only a monthly mail, we were for a long time perfectly unaware of this rising storm. But one of our friends in Washington cut from the newspapers nearly a hundred denunciatory extracts of us and sent them out to us.

"They arrived here one Sunday in the month of May, 1857, and I remember that, instead of religious exercises, we had those slips read at the tabernacle all day.

"The next we knew, a mail contract that we had purchased and had fully stocked with teams, stations, horses, and every appurtenance, at a cost of $300,000, and which was subsidized with only $20,000 a year, was taken from us at Washington and given to other parties for $100,000. That was a great blow to us. Had we been in communication with the eastern people more frequently and surely, they would never have made that war upon us.

"The next we knew, old General Harney had been placed in command of a great army to move against us.

"We hated Harney, because he had recently massacred a lot of Indian women, and was called among us 'the Squaw Killer.' Afterward, you know, he was removed, and Sidney Johnston substituted for him. We were determined Harney should not practice his bloody instincts upon us. I was appointed commander of our forces, and moved out by Weber and Echo Canons, and sent my scouting parties far ahead. We relied upon

the alliance of winter as a military friend, and everybody was united for resistance.

"Van Vliet, Quartermaster, came out to Salt Lake to see what ·he could get, in anticipation of the arrival of the army, in the way of supplies and quarters. We told him he should not have a shingle for shelter, a pound of bread, nor a bundle of fodder. He saw that he could make nothing out of us and departed. I had him followed almost to the Missouri River by day and night, and when he made his report I had men in his camp watching him there."

"For what distance and time did you harass that army, General Wells?"

"We were on their flank and in their rear almost all the time from their quitting the Missouri River till they got to Bridger. My orders were to hinder them in every way short of shedding blood, but I was not to kill anybody. And I never did. One of my skirmishing parties was captured, and upon the men were found copies of my orders, which were afterward printed in Washington city. Those instructions show conclusively that if I had killed anybody I would have disobeyed commands, and yet I am now indicted for the murder of a man named Yates, committed, as alleged, at that time, and upon the oath of a desperado who confesses to the murder of about twenty men committed by his own hand.

"On the contrary, my operations were confined to embarrassing the road, making panic and turning back teams. I thought that if I could retard the march, a more charitable and better informed public opinion would rise up in the East. I had a company of men in the rear of their teams which would arrest a certain number of teamsters every day, and after leaving them sufficient stores to regain their base of supplies, they were turned to the right about. But we found that they would merely go back until we ceased to watch them, and then return. So it became necessary to burn their teams and incapacitate them for a campaign. This was done north of Fort Bridger, on the Big and Little Sandy Rivers.

"Every night those troops encamped I had men among them. Their conduct showed significantly what they meant to do to us. They had doggerel songs, copies of which were captured, announcing their intention to make a barrack of Brigham Young's house, and enjoy his family. These songs inflamed our people, and united us as one man in the defense of our settlements.

"But just about this time the United States had some troubles nearer home, in Kansas, or somewhere. The fact is, Providence was in it. It was an interposition of Almighty God. The reinforcements from the East came up slowly, or were halted on the way, and the Administration at Washington, having reaped no glory and being subjected to considerable criticism, thought it prudent to compromise. They sent Senator Powell, of Kentucky, and Ben. McCulloch to us, in 1858, as Peace Commissioners, and we were offered a free pardon for all we had done if we would let the troops go through the form of passing through or by Salt Lake, not stopping or quartering here, but encamping out or beyond the city.

"We had done nothing except try to protect our property and the honor of our families, and now we were to accept a pardon.

"Some time after that Senator Broderick, of California, was here, and he told us the Government could have raised one million volunteer troops at that time, to wipe us out utterly. Such was to be our doom for protecting ourselves.

"To avoid bloodshed we consented to let a camp be formed within our territory, and the army marched by, encamping beyond the Jordan, then in Brigham's Canon, and finally at Camp Floyd. There they remained until 1861, when they destroyed stores, munitions and quarters and went off to take part in the war of the rebellion.

"Had these troops annoyed us we were prepared to cut every ditch, and fire every town and shelter in the Territory. Tinder had been placed in the houses and men systematically delegated to set it off."

"Where would you have gone, General Wells?"

"I don't know just where. We had provided for that, however."

"General Wells, have you any idea what inclination General Grant has in the matter of these prosecutions for polygamy?"

"Our advisers at Washington say that Grant has avowed his intention to execute either the Cragin or Cullom bills, if Congress will pass them, and if neither be passed, then he will execute the law of 1862."

"What reasons are there for his taking up polygamy at this critical time in the period of mining and railway development here?"

"Well, sir, our offense is like that of the Caffirs against the Dutch. The Caffirs said : 'Our greatest crime is that we have received a beautiful country from the Almighty, and you want it.'"

SALT LAKE AND UTAH PICTURES.

SALT LAKE, October 27.

HERE is the Territory of Utah, occupying to the Pacific coast very nearly the same situation that Ohio bears to the Atlantic States, suspended between a great lake and a great river, the Colorado, but many thousand feet above the sea. It is a solitary conquest from the desert, accomplished by the necessities of religious fanaticism; and it is nothing else, except certain mines and railways which availed themselves of the comfortable institutions of this settlement. The time seems to have come when the system of government which has prevailed here must meet with the two forces of resident democracy and a distant public opinion, the former antagonizing itself slowly and moving against Mormonism by attrition and with due regard to the preservation of property; the latter violent and unreasoning, and led on by emissaries even more violent and far less scrupulous.

This is the issue: Shall Mormonism fall by an attack of natural and social forces, to which its inherent weakness will make it an easy victim, or must it be the subject of a crusade, which will merely force it to shift its geography and retain the worst of its practices. In the one case we preserve Utah and its labor; in the other ordain a new lease of life to polygamy and extinguish a community in much admirable, and a settlement not to be restored.

So much attention has been paid to Salt Lake City by tourists and journalists that the Eastern public possess little or no idea of the other thriving towns and cities of Utah. From Brigham City to St. George, a distance of about three hundred and fifty miles, there is a chain of settlements reaching through Central Utah north and south, almost entirely. Mormon, and almost every large town contains a tabernacle and a tithing-house, and several a residence with family attached, for President Young. There are twenty counties in Utah, and all are connected by a road and telegraph system. The richest counties lie between Salt Lake City and the northern boundary, but the belt of the settlement follows the general line of the western slope of the Wahsatch Mountains and stops at St. George, on the river Virgin, while there are two good lateral valleys, one toward the head-waters of the Virgin, whose farther settlement to the east is Kanab Fort, and another in the San Pete Valley, where there are several rich settlements presided over by Orson Hyde. The San Pete Valley makes good wheat, and in it are the towns of Manti, Moram, Springfield, Mt. Pleasant and Ephraim, ranging from fifteen hundred to twenty-five hundred people each.

Southward from Salt Lake, the great road to Arizona runs parallel with the Jordan River, the outlet of Utah Lake into Salt Lake, leaving to the east the great Cottonwood mining district, and leading to Provo, which is, next to Salt Lake and Ogden, the most important place in the Territory. Provo stands upon the Timpon-ayos River, near Utah Lake, a clear, deep, fresh-water sheet, full of heavy trout, and it contains the best water power in the Territory. Here is Brigham's seven-story granite woolen mill. President Smart, ex-Mayor of Salt Lake, is the town authority. Passing Nephi and several other thrifty places, the road reaches Fillmore, ninety-six miles from Salt Lake, the real capital of the Territory by designation, and still showing the disused stone wing of an intended capital edifice. Below Fillmore, upon a "divide," is a telegraph operator, quartered in a stone fort to protect him from Indians, who are sometimes bad here. At Beaver, a town of two thousand one hundred people, forty miles south of Fillmore, one of the three United States District Courts is held. The next important place is Parowan, founded by Geo. A. Smith, in 1852, and then Cedar City, in a coal and iron region, with a deserted forge. Just south of this place we cross the rim of the great Salt Lake basin, and almost immediately the country turns red in color, and wears that wizard look as if scorched by fire. The first town beyond is Toquerville, founded in 1859; then the town of Washington, with six hundred inhabitants and Brigham's celebrated cotton mill. Finally, in the southwest corner of the Territory stands St. George, on the Rio Virgin, a town of tropical looking groves and neat cottages of wood, adobe and stone upon a plain between mountain "benches," the plain itself exuding glauber salts in places for acre upon acre, which must be covered with thousands of cartloads of sand, and drenched out by patient processes. This is, in many respects, the most remarkable and also most promising place in Utah; it is to Mormondom what Los Angeles in

California is to the North American; a grapery, cotton field, and invalid resort. Even here Brigham has a cot and family on the brink of Arizona. He has personally visited every part of this region, and at the age of sixty-nine he took Savage, the chief photographer here, upon a tour with him up the wild volcanic vale of the Virgin, and made him take views of the "Little Zion Valley," the Mormon Yosemite, where they expect to establish summer and winter resorts when the railway is finished.

Utah is equal to the New England States in area, but only one hundred and fifty thousand acres are under irrigation, and the capacity of the utmost irrigating system is limited to three hundred thousand acres more. Without running streams there can be no agriculture nor even reliable pastures here; the timber is sparse, small and difficult of access; the Indians were never able to get anything from the Territory, and the soil, although apparently rich, would relapse to dry gravel and clay in a month but for these needy and ever vigilant husbandmen. Utah, as it stands, is just capable of feeding the miners, merchants, troops and railroad gangs which have availed themselves of the Mormom occupation, and in this view Mormonism has been as lucky an episode in the course of empire as the discovery of gold in California or the inception of the Texan Republic. The tithing system, the absolute superintendence of the materialistic Brigham Young, and the semi-ecclesiastical discipline prevailing here, were as much the impositions of nature as of ambition; they are growing weaker now because the work is nearly performed. Hundreds of miles of canals and dikes, a people distributed over all the reclaimable region of the Territory, co-operation reduced from a religious duty to a voluntary and profitable system and upon a relative scale larger than elsewhere in the world,—these, no matter how they came about, are triumphs not to be gainsayed by the political economist and statesman, however the zealot and the prowling territorial politician may belittle them.

Utah, agriculturally, as nobody else but the Mormons could have developed it, is a necessity to the mining, railroad, and military operations of the central continent; for these enterprises subsist upon the produce of these farms, and a large human settlement here is also a strategic experiment. The neighboring mines of Idaho, Nevada, Montana and Colorado draw much of their store supplies from the valley.

"It isn't like Nevada," said a miner to me, yesterday; "here you can just walk down the mountain, from the mine to the foot, and find eggs, butter, and milk in the Mormon settlement."

The army and the railroads, moved from this point strategically, must also subsist upon Mormon agriculture. The time may come when the mines of the neighboring territories must be abandoned by reason of the cost of labor and living around them, but here agriculture and population had preceded mines and railways nearly a quarter of a century, and even under the present mining excitement mining labor costs only two dollars and a half a day, while in Nevada, barren of farms, it costs four dollars. It is largely Mormon labor which is completing the whole central railway system, striking out as boldly at present down the affluents of the Columbia and Colorado Rivers as it did upon the heavy work in Echo and Weber Canons for the Union Pacific Railway.

It is the opinion of many of the ablest men in the country that Utah will be the main manufacturing country for the Pacific Coast, like the Pittsburg region of the East. Already the manufactures here embrace cotton and woolen mills, iron, leather, flour, gloves, and small wares. The system of farming by irrigation is readily adaptable to water power uses. Coal is found just east of Salt Lake, which is used along eight hundred miles of the Pacific Railway, and other facts indicate Salt Lake as the emporium of all the business between the Rocky Mountains and the Sierra Nevada.

But what elements of population will take this soil and conduct agriculture here if the Mormons should abandon it? Gentiles tell me that between the drought, grasshoppers, alkali, the need of perpetual co-operation to regulate the ditches, and the primitive poverty of the ground, Mormon frugality and unity only can sustain the miracle of this garden in the desert. There are not five Gentile farmers in Utah. An exodus to Mexico, with their abundance of fine heads of cattle, sheep and horses, might give Mormonism a better empire, but what race would revive this one?

The probability of emigration is a widespread theme already, in view of the harsh attitude of the Courts here. Mormonism has been a series of emigrations, from Kirtland to Missouri, eight hundred miles; thence to Nauvoo, four hundred miles;

thence to Salt Lake, fifteen hundred miles; and each exodus has been an epoch and an advantage to the church. From St. George it is but four hundred miles across Arizona by a well defined and serviceable road to the Republic of Mexico, and there are settlements and military posts as far as Tucson and Tabac on the brink of Mexico. The Mexicans will welcome anywhere between Chihuahua and Sinaloa, these quiet settlers who can create a power on the Gulf of California, and curb the Apaches by either the Quaker or the Crook method.

I have already informed you that the proposition to emigrate was debated on the first of October, in the business office of Brigham Young, and that there were present, besides the three members of the First Presidency, the majority of the Twelve Apostles and many of the Seventies and Bishops, in all upwards of thirty persons, the sinew of the Church. Had the proposition been carried out, Utah would have been systematically desolated and rendered incapable of supporting ten thousand people, and private vengeance would have been an episode of so vast and bitter an act of sacrifice and despair.

The remarkable man who presides over these people added to the many conquests of his life, the final victory over his absolute spirit when he put by the counsels of his elders and went into court upon an indictment which, in its language and tone, is at variance with whatever is known of his life by any third party. Brigham Young is just as guilty of "lewd and licentious conduct and cohabitation" as the Viceroy of Egypt, the Chief of the Cherokees, the Emperor of Ja-

pan, or the patriarch Moses, with their several wives. His children and wives are all acknowledged and provided for; of the latter he has sixteen, and of children sixty odd. His offense is polygamous marriages, practised for twenty years with the full knowledge of an unbroken series of United States officials, Judges and Presidents included, by all of whom he has been treated with equality, and by many with distinction. The statute under which he is indicted was passed by Mormons in their Territorial Legislature, and made punishable by from three to ten years' imprisonment, at the time of the formation of their code, and it was meant to apply to common fornication. There is but one statute in the same terms in any State code,—that of Massachusetts, passed in 1790; and this, as construed, provides that the lewdness and lasciviousness must be public, and that secret cohabitation is not intended; in other words, the offense is against decency and not chastity. There has been no complaint of this nature ever made in the present instance, but the Judge and the Prosecuting Attorney, the *avant guard* of that supposititious distant sentiment, *packed* a grand jury—there is no other word applicable—to indict Young, and will pack a petit jury to convict him. In my opinion, and in the apprehension of every business man and military officer in Utah, if this is done, and Brigham Young be sent to jail, the Church authorities, including himself, will not be able to prevent an outbreak or an exodus. If he should die in the hands of the authorities, being old and of proud spirit, the Church will have a greater martyr than Joseph Smith to win disciples upon, and in any event, the roaming Seventies will have a new illustration and provocation for zeal.

If President Young were indicted upon a charge of bigamy or polygamy, instead of lasciviousness and lewdness, he would do well to stand up in Court and plead guilty. His indictment on the head alleged is preposterous and merely tantalizing. As to the later indictment for murder, on the affidavit of Bill Hickman before the grand jury, that is a graver matter and deserves a paragraph of consideration

The necessities of Mormonism have always demanded a mingling of military with civil stringency. Driven away from civilization, amongst Indians and "Greasers," they were required to maintain troops, and they even indulged the hope that the land they occupied might be purchased or conquered by them from Mexico. Among their motley converts were many rough characters from Missouri, Illinois, and Iowa, and as they retreated from civilization with the method and order of Xenophon, they put to temporary use and importance some of these physical bravos who are now swearing off their own old personal atrocities against the heads of the Mormon Church, who have "cut them off."

The vilest of these fellows is Bill Hickman, a Judas and a Joab in one. He was under indictment for murder, when the United States Government befriended him, and accepted his irresponsible statement that Brigham Young's son, Joseph—an able, but not always temperate or judicious young man—had said that one Yates ought to be put out of the way. This is hearsay evidence, and it is all that the Court possesses. Hickman is a Missouri border ruffian, a po-

lygamist, and a human hyena. General Morrow told me at Camp Douglas that Bill Hickman was unworthy of credit or companionship. Hickman admits having murdered Yates, with his own hand, in 1857.

Another crime charged to Brigham Young is the "Mountain Meadow Massacre," so called—an act of retaliation and rapacity, committed sixteen years ago, in Southwestern Utah, by one John D. Lee, since "cut off" from the church. Lee led a band of Indians and Mormons into the camp of these emigrants, and slew them for their stock, and for revenge. It was a bad deed, but if it is to be recalled and adjusted in the Courts, it should not be Bill Hickman, but some of the parties or witnesses to the crime, who should be brought forward to give testimony concerning it.

Human life in Utah is safer than probably anywhere in civilization. The motives and causes of murder exist in a less degree—as avarice, liquor, gambling, quarrelsomeness and prostitution. The industrious political vagabonds who write letters from Utah to the East have created the band of "Danites" and other hobgoblins out of air and foolscap.

I talked to Porter Rockwell, the alleged leader of the "Danites," a fat, curly-haired, good-natured chap, fond of a drink, a talk, and a wild venture. The United States authorities have several times used him to make arrests of lawless characters.

Among the Mormons are bad people; polygamy and ignorance are no guarantee against the corruptions of original sin; but Mormonism is a religion, essentially the two testaments of Judaism and Christianity, with

Joseph Smith's gibberish appended, and the sincere believers in it find no warrant for murder anywhere in their creed.

The loyalty of the Mormons toward the United States is also made the subject of accusation. I am writing these letters for people whom I respect, and not for small fry, and the former class know very well that Mormonism has never had great reason to admire the United States. We are dealing now with a phenomenon, a superstition, and have got to look at it to know how to apprehend it and govern it. Begotten among us, in the Empire State, near the head of the Ohio Valley, this church is a native dispensation, a gospel prepared for the new world, attempting to recite the story of our origin and that of the Indians, our predecessors. In my belief, it was less the offspring of imposture than of disease. Such as it is, it relies upon the common basis of Christian orthodoxy—faith! You must embrace it not only by reason, but by the abnegation of reason. You must begin at the end and embrace it in the old-fashioned Whitfieldian way of paroxysm. It is almost solely an Anglo-Saxon church. What is absurdest in it is nearest the theology of the religions our fathers believed in. Moses took the Gospel on stone; Joe Smith on gold. Both told the rise, exodus and power, and prophesied the discomfiture of a nation. I do not, personally, believe one figment of Mormonism as a story. I do, without cavil or question, believe the whole story of Moses and Christ; because I know nothing else; that was my hearthstone faith; I inherit it and its civilization. Among the mature fruits of that civilization are forbearance,

the belief that error is mortal, and a reasonable education. The human mind and our race have risen to mighty fermentations and heroisms, upon propositions as absurd and astonishing as Joseph Smith's. Here is the greatest Territory of the Union erected upon a delusion. Let the creation itself smother the delusion. Give society a chance and it will drive polygamy back into the vices. Society, under its political organization, has been able by mild emulation to reduce ecclesiasticism to docility. Methodism at one period adopted a disciplinary system of brotherhood, under which a man like Judge McKean might have ruled every Methodist off a jury in cases affecting his fellow-Methodist. Quakerism was a revolt and a rebuke against the civil establishments of its time. English Puritanism, as it ruled in New England, coalesced the congregation and the town, the spiritual and the civil arm. These theologies survive, shorn of their physical and intolerant pretensions. They have their trophies and their better results. In the same way, Mormonism was an ignorant attempt to make a State out of a church, a magistracy out of a priesthood. It has learned that it cannot escape from society. The temporal power of the church is already reduced. Shall we go back into the dark and desert age of Mormonism to try and punish it for its excrescences? Shall we bring up the Society which hanged the witches, the Quaker who interrupted a church meeting, and the Mormon who tried to create an army to protect his church, and deal with them like reasonable criminals? Six months ago, before Judge McKean arrived here, like a Catholic Jesuit dropping down in the vale of the wilderness, the Mormons were thoroughly reconciled to the United States and anxious for its benefits. Their past persecutions were forgotten. It is we, or our inquisitorial Courts, who have recalled together our aggressions and the Mormons' excesses.

Let us be cool-headed, and not jump behind our century! Polygamy is the least mortal of institutions. It was an afterthought of Mormonism. Democracy will wrestle with it presently and crush the life out of it. We need not sentimentalize over it, like that short-haired show-woman, Miss Anna Dickinson, who is in no danger. Polygamy is merry enough to read about in the Arabian Nights and in Byron's or Morris's poems. We construe it into a terror and move upon it with serious faces, because our own neighbors and kinsmen are fooling with the folly.

Co-operation, advocated by the press and reformers as a benefit everywhere else, had no sooner been adopted among the Mormons than there went up a howl of " monopoly," " commercial restriction!"

To get at the bottom of this matter, I went right to William Jennings, the richest Mormon, Brigham excepted, and who was alleged to have been compelled by Brigham to give his store to the enterprise. Mr. Jennings inhabits a large and beautiful house, which probably cost two hundred thousand dollars, and he dispenses cheer of a hearty and vinous quality. He has but one wife living, and his daughters expressed themselves indignantly that their deceased mother was to be declared impure and themselves illegitimate by a Court of Judges belonging to another religion.

Mr. Jennings said that he lived in Missouri, at St. Joseph, and was not a member of the church, nor cognizant of its existence, when he left England. The plan of the co-operation store was Brigham Young's, and he proposed it as early as 1853, but Jennings, Lawrence, Walker Brothers and Godby, to whom it was suggested, did not think favorably of it. These merchants made large sums of money — sums out of proportion to the producer and consumer — in consideration of brotherly equity. Wheat was bought from the Mormon farmers at seventy-five cents a bushel, often paid for in merchandise, and then sold in the form of flour in the mining regions for twenty-five dollars gold per hundred weight, a profit of several hundred per cent.

"Thus," said Mr. Jennings, " we all prospered inordinately, and I had meditated retiring from business in 1867, when again President Young revived his plan of a co-operation store. Those of us who intended to remain steadfast to the Church found it now imperative to agree, because a certain squatter here, named McGroarty, had managed to get about one-twentieth of the vote of the people in Utah, and he had been sent up to Congress by Walker Brothers, and others, with money made out of our people, to contest the seat of our delegate, W. H. Hooper. It was apparent that these fortunes made among us were to be played against the dignity and will of the people. I at once rented my store for five years to the co-operation society, and took $75,000 worth of stock, a larger amount than any-

6

body else, although President Young is now nearly equal with me in the concern. We made the thing democratic, so that five dollars would constitute a stockholder, and we tightened it only with regard to the transferral of shares; for if this Court up here could by any means entrap us into its precincts, we should have injunctions, receivers and mandamuses without stint. The capital is not far from half a million, and we pay ten per cent. a month, so that our customers who are stockholders get their proportion in dividends. We have brought down prices to our poor people who are not stockholders, and Mr. Clawson, the manager, seeks to regulate profits down to ten per cent. upon articles of prime necessity.

"While the co-operative store has been a gratifying and beneficent success, other merchants are doing a large, independent business. Mormons are free to buy anywhere, and their only incentive to go to the ' co-op' is interest. We have only one branch which we directly control, at Ogden, but our plan is imitated in every ward of Salt Lake, and in every settlement of Utah."

Speaking of Godby, Mr. Jennings said that he was flighty and ambitious, and that he had done a mean thing in taking a fifth wife after apostatizing. " No man has a right to be a polygamist," said Mr. Jennings, " unless he believes in it as a revelation."

Not only is monogamy the practice of the entire " Josephite " or Young Smith school of the Mormon Church, but even at Salt Lake it has exemplars, such as Fermamorz Little and William Jennings, who are considered the richest men in the Territory

next to Brigham Young. Jennings at one time had two wives, but since the death of the first he has never re-married. These men are probably worth one million dollars apiece, and worth half as much is W. H. Hooper, Mormon banker and Delegate in Congress, also a monogamist in practice and prejudice. Bolivar Roberts, who is very rich in real estate, and who is reputed to have received three hundred thousand dollars for his interest in the Sweetwater Mine, is likewise the Mormon husband of one wife. John T. Caine, editor of the *Salt Lake Herald*, the leading newspaper between Denver and Sacramento; D. E. Calder, Superintendent of the Utah Central Railroad; H. T. Fantz, and many others, find the cares of one family sufficient.

Polygamy, however, is warmly defended, even by Mormon monogamists, as right, if not convenient. John Young, the son of Brigham, has three wives, and Joseph Young, jr., two, while two pairs of Brigham's daughters are married respectively to H. B. Clawson and —— ——.

Brigham Young's most noted wife is called Amelia; she is a vivacious, spirited woman, about thirty-two years old, American born, and without children. Another of the President's wives is Mrs. Decker, who retains indications of much former beauty, and her daughters are the handsomest of Brigham's children. The old gentleman looks out well for avocations for his sons-in-law, and it is said that in his will he has divided all his property into seven hundred shares, given the bulk of it to the church, and distributed the rest equally among his families.

I saw Brigham at the Social Hall, on the occasion of my last visit here, bid four of his wives adieu. The old gentleman had been dancing, but had fatigued the legs of seventy years, and he approached the cluster of his helpmates, buttoned up in a blue overcoat with a white vest underneath, a red woolen comforter around his neck, and a worn silk hat in his hand. He looked very large, square, and bland, and he said with tenderness and dignity, shaking each by the hand:

"My dear, I bid you good night!"

The wives crowding up, with apparent emulation, asked if it was his wish that they also should accompany him home.

"No," said Brigham, "stay as long as you please. I will have the carriage come back and wait for you at the door below. Good night!"

They were all middle-aged women, common-place but cheerful; Brigham is said to object to *his* wives dancing round dances. It is wonderful that a Mormon with half a dozen wives can be jealous or fastidious about each of them, and yet I have heard people here fly into a passion because their *wives* were spoken to on the street by strangers, or stared at. The only case of assassination chargeable with any degree of probability to the Mormons, was that of Brassfield, a teamster, shot dead in the streets of Salt Lake for selling a Mormon's furniture and proposing to elope upon the proceeds of it with a wife.

Godby, who hates Brigham Young sincerely, has four wives, besides one divorced. Since he has been "cut off" from the church he has contemplated setting the example of radical monogamy. "And yet," says Godby, "I love all my wives so equally, and they all love me so harmoniously, that I cannot pick out the one to stay nor those who must go."

This same Godby, in a speech upon the inviolability of plural marriages, which he made some time ago, gave in the language of the resolution a remarkable concession made by the Board of Orthodox Missionaries in India. It was a question as to what those Hindoos who had been married to several wives before their conversion, should do about them after baptism, repentance, &c., and admission into the Christian Church.

Looking at the distresses and awkwardnesses of the situation on all sides, the missionaries agreed that polygamous converts might retain those wives which they already possessed, and go on as before.

With this precedent—the only one consistent with humane principles—we may ask how much harder our Methodist brethren are going to be upon these many children of many wives born into the world under the sacred presumption of an inviolable marriage? Reverse the situation! Be the Mormon, and with your families before you, designate those to be sacrificed, bastardized and disowned!

INSIDE VIEWS OF UTAH SOCIETY.

SALT LAKE, Oct. 27.

Mr. Kinzer, a Californian, who has been developing mines in Southern Utah, told me several anecdotes which illustrate Mormon dignity and sincerity. One day, as the period of the semi-annual Mormon conference approached, he met a very old woman driving a cart to which an ox was attached. The miner peeped into her cart and saw that it contained nothing to eat except a little salt meat and a bag of meal, with fodder for the ox. This was somewhere in Juab County.

"Old lady," said the miner, "where are you going?"

"Up to our conference, sir. I ha'n't been there now for two year, but I want to get my soul warmed up a little. It appeared as if I could not stay away any longer. I have been in church twenty-two years, and I always go to the conference when I can, but I live 'way down here on the Santa Clara River, and it takes me three weeks to go to Salt Lake."

This poor old zealot had actually been more than two weeks on the way to her church conference; she camped out every night, and was entirely alone and unbefriended. The miners gave her some cheese and bread and sent her on her way rejoicing.

The Mormon conferences are fearfully apostolical. Twelve thousand people often attend them. A band of music plays at the Tabernacle gate as the Saints go in and as they come out, and "Shoo Fly," "Bully for You," "High Ricketty Barlow," &c., are the class of tunes selected. Go into that vast enclosure, and you will see the Mormon Church conducting its business, the hands of its officials held up by the whole broad public sentiment. W. H. Hooper told me that for nearly twenty years he had attended these conferences, and he had never heard a half dozen nays voted against any measure propounded by the High Quorum. Brigham Young reads such an announcement as this:

"Brother William Johnson is nominated for a mission to Russia of two years, at his own expense. All in favor of that nomination will say aye."

A roar goes up from the great conference of Saints, and Brother William Johnson, who perhaps keeps a shop in one of the streets of Salt Lake, who does not speak any language but his own, and that indifferently well, and who has never traveled away from home ten miles in his life, has no option but to hearken to that cry as if it were as sacred as the voice in St. Paul's dream of "Come over into Macedonia and help us."

A great many people who read this will cry out, "Despotism," but I, who am a preacher's son in the Methodist Church, have seen the heart of my mother sink down when my father was ordered off, by government as absolute as Brigham Young's, to live two years in some swampy part of the earth for such a salary as could be picked up,—marriage fees and presents of sausage and sparerib about Christmas thrown in.

The death of Brigham Young will be, as things stand, a benefit to his people. Of Brigham's devotion, credulity and constancy as a Mormon there can be no doubt. He is as sincere a man in his church as Bishop

Simpson is in the Methodist Church or Judge McKean in his. But the old man has been cramped up in Utah since 1848. Absolute authority has made him vain; want of travel to distant parts has kept his charity from expanding. To him, the whole earth lies under the thatch of the Wahsatch Mountains, and he is only aware of the fearful mightiness of democratic sentiment in America from the few troops camped in his vicinity, from the miserable character of the Federal officials who go out there to blackmail him, and from the stream of respectful visitors, for whom he holds a levee every morning, and who butter him with praises, while perhaps the same people are inditing letters to the East raising a hue and cry against his Empire. He will leave behind him in that State a name never to be rivaled in the future prosperous history of Utah. This very old man, against whom the Courts are battering, and who may soon be a fugitive on the borders of Arizona to avoid the penitentiary of Salt Lake,—I dare believe the fame of Brigham Young is as indissolubly bound in the literature and reverence of the Rocky Mountain people, as the names of La Salle, John Winthrop and Hernando Cortez are embedded in other parts of the country.

I was talking one day with a distinguished apostle of the Mormon Church, and he used this curious illustration :

"Suppose, Mr. Townsend," he said, "that Joseph Smith had been born 3400 years ago, and Moses in the year 1800, A. D., thus reversing the order of their several revelations,—which would be the harder to believe?"

I replied : "You ask me too much. I am not familiar with the story of Moses. My notion of Moses is obtained from one of Michael Angelo's statues ; he always seemed to me to be a fair man."

"Now," said this apostle, the story of Joseph Smith is, that he discovered a set of golden plates, and he was divinely endowed to translate them. You ask where are those plates? We answer that Joseph Smith gave them back to the angel, who kept them. Moses on the other hand went up into Mount Sinai, taking no witnesses with him, and is alleged to have had a familiar talk with the Lord. The Lord gave him two tablets of stone on which the commandments are engraved ; but Moses never showed the people those stone tablets, any more than Joseph Smith showed the golden plates. When Moses came down from Sinai with the tablets, he found the people worshipping a golden calf, and it says in the ninth chapter of Deuteronomy, that he cast down the tablets and broke them to pieces. Then he went up into the mountain again, as the tenth chapter of Deuteronomy discloses and was permitted by the Lord, to hew himself a new set of tablets, on which the commandments were engraved, these tablets were put into the ark, and they were everlastingly concealed from the public eye. Now had Moses been named Joseph Smith, the gentile world would have scoffed at this story, and would have said that the nonappearance of the stone tablets, the breaking of the original pair, and the re-engraving of an imitation by the prophet himself, were all subterfuges such as those which accompanied the chiseling of the Cardiff giant.

But you have had preached at you for eighteen hundred years, the legend of Moses, and you take it without question while you laugh at the altogether more consistent story of the translation of the golden plates. Both instances must be accepted by faith and not by reason. Our people out here believe equally in the tale of Moses, and in that of Joseph, and you who accept one half of the gospel, want to put us in jail and break us up for believing the other half. You came in here just like the Catholic priests got into the vales of the Waldenses. Failing to convert us or rather to unconvert us, you begin to persecute us. It is no fault of ours that we offend you; for we left civilization fifteen hundred miles behind us, in order not to irritate you. We think that our revelation treats of matters if possible more important to human nature than the Old Testament. It solves the problem of the past history of America. It has the only new gospel and indigenous prophet and seer on this hemisphere. It has grown more rapidly than the Jewish power, and if it were not for our notion on the subject of marriage, I believe we would have more converts in the United States, than any other sect.

"Mormon Utah is a congregation of all the good institutions which you separately maintain. It is a house of correction, an inebriate asylum, an almshouse, a church, an intelligence office, a system of apprenticeship, a commission of emigration, a loan office, a college of agriculture, a school of mines and manufactures; in short it collects from all parts of the earth, the weak, the ignorant, and those who need spiritual and social reformation, and brings them out here removed from temptation and constructs them into a useful citizency."

This is a case arising under Judge McKean's system of ruling Mormons off a jury in civil as well as criminal trials affecting them in any way. Engelbrecht, a liquor seller, refused to take out a city license, (the licenses here being costly, $300 a month to sell spirits over a bar; $200 a month to sell liquors wholesale and retail, not to be drank on the premises; $100 a month to keep a wholesale liquor store; $50 a month to sell ale and beer,) and after being notified of the consequences by the Justice of the Peace in his ward, one Clinton, the liquors of Engelbrecht were poured into the street. He sued Clinton and the officers of the corporation for malicious destruction of his stock, under a territorial statute, making malicious damage punishable three times the value of the property destroyed. McKean ruled every Mormon off the jury on the ground of bias and incapability of giving a verdict according to the evidence. The liquor seller won the case by the packed jury, and for nineteen thousand dollars worth of liquors got an award of fifty-seven thousand dollars. The case is to be carried up to the Supreme Court and pressed for a decision in advance of its order, on the ground that this wholesale and indiscriminate trial of cases affecting the great majority of the people by juries selected from an insignificant minority, is subversive of justice in Utah, and puts the liberty and property of the people at the disposal of two men—the majority of the Court. The Mormons have a superstitious faith in the honesty of the Supreme Court of Washington, but they regard the Supreme Court of Utah as a mixture of fanaticism, dullness and draw-poker. If it be decided at Washington that McKean's way of making up juries is legal, the Mormons will quietly submit, but it is not probable that the Supreme Court, even as manipulated within the past two years, will indorse this brutal manner of violating the essential spirit of trial by jury.

In Utah, as generally in the Territories, the Federal administration is loose, discordant and slip-shod. The late Prosecutor, Hempstead, was hated by McKean, for objecting to the jury-packing system, and the present Prosecutor is appointed by the Court only; the post military commanders are invariably friendly with the Mormons, because they perceive nothing admirable or lovable in the Federal officials. Judge Strickland frequently smokes cigars and whittles sticks while holding court. A vague impression, started by the preacher "Doctor" Newman, that Grant wants a general movement made on polygamy, an ambrosial notoriety seeker, he devised a trip to Utah many months ago, and the Mormons, in Democratic fairness, threw open their tabernacle to him to let him say the worst against their theology. Imagine a Methodist Bishop giving up his pulpit to a Mormon in like circumstances. Newman now returns the courtesy of the Mormons by setting on foot, through the President, this whole precipitate assize against polygamy. Thus are schemes of statesmanship balked by theological pretenders, and shallow preachers are given the scope and influence of Cardinals like Richelieu and Antonelli.

Bates, who has been appointed United States Attorney for Utah within the past few days, is a burnt-out Chicago lawyer, a friend of Lyman Trumbull, and a conservative man. We shall probably hear no more of Basking's ferocious billingsgate, where he called Brigham Young a thief, assassin, &c., before the smiling Judge McKean, and reduced the associations even of the livery stable where the United States Court is held.

Senator Trumbull says these prosecutions are out of all equity, and that they should be stopped, and polygamy left to its natural enemies, prosperity, Gentile influx, opinion and competition.

There is no doubt that the successor of Brigham Young is already resolved upon by that old Moses himself, and that he is advised of his nomination. It is George A. Smith, cousin to Joseph Smith, and the Historian of the Church, and also at present one of the three members of the "First Presidency."

A man more unlike Brigham Young it would be difficult to conceive. Brigham is the incarnation of will and purpose, a materialist, a Yankee Turk. George A. Smith is the spirit of reverence, gentleness and accord, and in his hands Mormonism will cease to offend its neighbors, and resolve to a quiet, docile, but still numerous and proselytizing body of worshipers. Smith is very little of a polygamist. He has none of Brigham's consideration for money and clearheadedness upon the great unit of the interest-bearing dollar. Smith is one of us literary folks, a man of the stamp of Thackeray, Peter Force and Washington Irving—

not equal to them in degree, perhaps, but in nature the same—a *collaborateur*, lover of traditions and family reminiscences, and a pleasing, dignified *raconteur* and politician. He has no avarice, no love of war, no vindictiveness, and he is yet a sincere, hale, immovable Mormon, believing in Joseph's revelations without question. I am told that there is no historical society in any county or State of the Union so perfectly complete in archives as that of the Mormons. The recording angel might have gone off on a holiday as far as they are concerned; for George A. Smith has kept the account for him.

And yet, this lolling, easy Bohemian has energies of his own not to be despised, and Brigham Young is more frequently in his society than with any of the Madames Young. He has a wonderful memory, power of language and stump-speaking, and adroit political management. He loves politics and is not a bigot. The Mormons have a weakness for the Smith family as the Islamites might have for the relatives of Mohammed, and there never was any Smith with more sagacity and *bonhommie* than this one. He is a very large, heavy, and self-enjoying man in appearance—resembling ex-Senator Toombs, of Georgia, but without Toombs' opinionatedness or passion. He weighs as much as Brigham Young, wears a brownish auburn wig and spectacles, walks with a cane, and has a ready smile and a big mouth to spread it upon. Although having two or three wives, I dare believe that George Smith is at heart a chaste, tender, and religious husband, father, friend and gentleman.

Here I close my letter for the present.

In conclusion, it must be said, seriously, warningly, to the Mormon leaders, that they must, by the force of example and edict, stop this policy of polygamy! They are to a very great extent still the "guides, philosophers and friends" of their masses. Let them put their flourishing territory in accord with the surrounding civilized populations, take domestic example from the white man's one wife, and not from the Indian's many squaws, and be, like a New Testament bishop, "the husband of one!" Let them bring Utah into the Union as a State, rid themselves of a judiciary and Governor responsible only to a distant public opinion, and share in the profits and comforts of an expanding, a developing, and a rich nation. Of what avail are industry and polygamy yoked together, the one slaving for the other to live ahungered upon its proceeds? Even President Young's millions will go thinly around among his numerous progeny. The present conflict between the United States and the polygamous leaders may be staved off, but similar troubles will arise again and again. The nation will not put up with polygamy much longer. Governments and administrations may keep hands off, but the danger to polygamy is from the power that makes administrations and governments—the Democratic populace, the public opinion. The very courts and troops now so obnoxious in Utah may one day be the refuge of the Mormon people, and that necessity for refuge will be when the public opinion catches up and overtakes the United States Government and supersedes it, as it did at Nauvoo. Heaven deliver a poor, thrifty and sincere people from that fate, and let Heaven make useful for this purpose the present leaders of the Mormon Church, so that we may see Utah saved from desolation.

A way seems to arise by which—as under our free system such communications should be brought about—the Mormon Church, the Mormon people, and the true course of law, justice and tolerance, may be secured. It was proposed at Salt Lake, to several Mormons in my presence, by a distinguished member of the church.

Namely : That the Mormon chiefs should not trifle with time, nor hesitate upon the brink of danger in this age of breech-loaders and volunteer soldiering. Let them dismiss the freak of an exodus to some other Territory, where in a few years the storm against polygamy will burst forth again. A forcible resistance, in my judgment, they never contemplated. Let them believe that many thousands of Gentiles take pride and interest in their past energy and useful acquisitions, and desire to see them protected in both and in their worship. But polygamy is not only a tenet ; it is a practice, and it encounters the whole force of the creed and current of the common law of civilization. Here is a way to deal with it, extinguish it, and make a wholesome and flourishing State out of an anomaly.

Let a convention be called promptly, even at once, before Congress gets well under way with next session's business. Let this convention prepare a State constitution and concede polygamy in return for the right of local government, trial by jury, and a share in the benefits of representation in the nation. If necessary to the dignity and conscience of the Mormon people, let them throw in their preamble or codicil the responsibility for abandoning polygamy in future upon the government they petition, and concede it to the cause of peace and the prejudice of the times. The country will not be unjust enough to demand them to violate the duties of paternity and wedlock in marriages already contracted, where the complaint does not arise within the marriage relation. Let them staunchly, inviolably agree and bind themselves to keep the agreements of this State constitution as they make it, and to attest the same, let them make the oath to sustain monogamous marital fidelity in all future marriages, a portion of the official oath to be taken by every State officer.

This concession will be statesmanship and sacrifice together on the part of those influential apostles, counselors and quorums who will bring it about. They will approve themselves worthy to preserve the State they have erected, and remove the last cause of interference with the civil rights and freedom of worship and faith. They will share in the benefits of a State to which they are already bound by the ties of race, interest, and neighborhood, and will find compensation for the loss of polygamy in riches, respect and stability. They will save themselves, by a speedy movement of this kind, from such political neutralization, I might say annihilation, as has overtaken the South. For, if they do not heed the warning, it may be too late. One rash act, the folly of any wretch, may blot out Utah politically, materially, ecclesiastically, even as a tradition ! " Now is the accepted time, and now is the day of salvation !"

THE END.

www.ingramcontent.com/pod-product-compliance
Lightning Source LLC
Chambersburg PA
CBHW032118080426
42733CB00008B/982